Rituals

for a

Peaceful Transition

Ford Boyer

BoRupp Productions/Starfire Servers
Alameda, California

ISBN: 0-7596-5486-7 (e-book)
ISBN: 0-7596-5487-5 (Paperback)

This book is printed on acid free paper.

Cover and photographs by Ford Boyer

Printed in the United States of America

Published in conjunction with:
BoRupp Productions/Starfire Servers
3327 Cook Lane
Alameda, CA 94502
fo4rd@attbi.com

1stBooks - rev. 07/5/02

This book is gratefully dedicated to:

Roxanne Boyer Waller

Jerry Cowley

Bob Galyean

Ben Carmines

All those who have suffered and died

and

Those who are still suffering and dying

Acknowledgements

My deepest gratitude to **Juelle Ann** my traveling companion during this incarnation (and probably many others), who does so much for so many and asks so little in return.

Lloyd Patterson, formerly of KRON-TV San Francisco, my ever present mentor who, using patience and loving understanding, firmly prods me onward.

To all those with whom I have worked and continue to work, especially those HIV/AIDS and Hospice clients who have taught me so much about living and dying.

A special thanks to my reader, Rigdzin Donna Caird, for her valuable insights and suggestions.

Some of the material in this book has been paraphrased, or directly quoted, from the Ageless Wisdom as written in the books by Alice A. Bailey. Permission to quote has been granted by the following:

Lucis Publishing Company, 120 Wall Street, 24th Floor, New York, NY 10005 for quotes from the Alice A. Bailey books.

A Course in Miracles, Foundation for Inner Peace, P. O. Box 1104, Glen Ellen, CA 95442

Alcoholic Anonymous, A. A. World Services, Inc., 475 Riverside Drive, New York, NY 10115

The Philosophy of Death and Dying, Himalayan International Institute of Yoga Science & Philosophies, RR1, Box 400, Honesdale, PA 18431

Table of Contents

CHAPTER Page

Acknowledgements v

Preface xiii

Prelude xvii

Chapter One: A Healthy Skepticism 1

Chapter Two: Connectedness 7

Ritual No. 1: 18

Chapter Three: The Soul and Crisis 25

Ritual No. 2 28

Chapter Four: Consciousness 34

Ritual No. 3 38

Chapter Five: Death 41

Ritual No. 4 42

Ritual No. 5 49

Chapter Six: It's the Law 55

Ritual No. 6 62

References 67

Learn to keep focussed in the head through visualization and meditation and through the steady practice of concentration; develop the capacity to live increasingly as the king seated on the throne between the eyebrows. This is a rule that can be applied to the everyday affairs of life.

Alice A. Bailey

Preface

Many books and articles have been written covering the subjects of mind, ritual, crisis, meditation, the terminally ill, and death and dying. The idea for this book came about as the result of my work with HIV/AIDS clients who are in varying stages of the disease.

At times, the subject of suicide and alternative measures to end the suffering of death arises. On several occasions, clients have commented that there should be some method of dying, a ritual maybe, available for those not interested in suicide, but wishing to make the death transition more understandable and comfortable.

At the prodding of several clients and recognizing the need for information that could be of immediate assistance to those who consider alternatives, I combined my psychological and spiritual knowledge and arrived at the subject matter of this book.

Due to the wide range of literacy within the reader population, I have used terminology appropriate for the average reader. Those who are ill or in the process of dying do not wish to plod through highly scientific or philosophizing language. Therefore, I have attempted to make the language as simple as possible.

Just as there is a wide range of readers, so there is a wide range of thinking on the subjects of the mind, ritual, crisis resolution, death and dying. This thinking has been built up over the centuries leading to an undue attachment to the physical aspect of life. It is the emphasis on the physical that creates the greater portion of sorrow and pain surrounding death and crises.

One of the purposes in preparing this book is to shatter some old forms of thinking about crisis and death and suggest some new concepts and rituals for the implementation of new thinking.

New thinking is needed because the word crisis has gained a "bad rap" and continues to do so. Whatever the reason, the average individual interprets a crisis as a negative occurrence.

Consequently, people want to escape temporarily from, or avoid altogether, life's daily crises. There is no denying that life could be simpler and more comfortable; however, we all face crises. And life continues, doesn't it?

What is it that allows some people to continue to plunge through life solving crisis after crisis and remain happy while others live an unhappy, crisis-ridden life? Facing crises is the most effective method for personal, group, national and international growth. It is through the facing and solving of crises that you continue to exist in physical bodies on planet Earth.

Prelude

I was sitting with a young man of 32 who was dying of AIDS. His eyes were open, turning upward occasionally, but he was not seeing his physical environment. He was looking at an inner realm of life as though he was searching for something or someone. I knew he could hear what was being said and I asked if he would like me to tell him a story. His hand, which was lying on top of mine, made a slight squeeze. This is what I told him.

....

There was a young man living on a far distant planet who decided to go on an adventure. He prepared himself for a long journey and boarded his space ship.

He investigated each star he passed and as time and distance passed, he saw in the distance a bright blue star twinkling in a manner somewhat differently from those around it. He decided that's where he would go.

Upon arriving, he noted that it was a planet tinged with blue and green and some white something or other moving over the surface. He decided to land. He landed his ship in a secluded place making sure he would remember where it was in case he needed it. His instrumentation indicated that the star was habitable but that he would need a different type of body in order to survive. He desired, and knowing that energy follows thought and desire, he found himself in a confining watery substance.

Much later, he was aware of bright lights and an unknown sound being emitted from his body. But, at least he felt free of the confining space. He had been born on Earth.

As he grew, he learned that he had something called parents. They fed and clothed him and sent him to a place called school. He learned about the planet he was on; a planet called Earth. He learned that the white substance high above him was called clouds and that sometimes the clouds poured down rain or ice or snow.

He learned about relationships, about prejudices and hatreds, joy and love. He learned about something called money and how his family saved, spent and squabbled over it. He learned about wars and battles and peace and quiet. He learned about sports and he especially loved to run with the wind. He ran up hills and down, through parks and towns. He learned about creating and became a designer. He learned what it meant to “make it on his own.”

He learned about sex and how it could grab and hold one in its clutches. He learned how it could bring on heartbreak and disease. He learned that he could love someone, and he did. He was young, in his late twenties, carefree and living life.

And then, he began to change. Something was happening to his body. His energy gave out much quicker and he often had trouble breathing. He was told that he was terminally ill and would not live much longer.

He put his life in order as best he could and walked slowly toward his ship. He knew he could no longer stay on Earth; he wanted to go home. Boarding his ship, he looked longingly at the beautiful planet he had come to love. As the ship moved swiftly away from Earth he looked back only one time, one quick glance. He knew he had learned all he could about life on Earth this trip and maybe he would be able to come back again in the future.

As he neared his home planet, he realized he would have to shed the bodies he had collected on Earth. Slowly, very slowly, he became aware that he was no longer attached to his physical body. He was feeling freer and lighter. The closer he came to home, another body was detached; that of the emotions, those strange sensations so dominant on Earth. Finally, he realized he was settling down on his home planet, free of all Earth's attachments, and his mind was crystal clear. As he moved through the door of his ship, he recognized familiar minds waiting to welcome him and he was filled with joy and peace. He knew that he had earned a long rest and that he would have plenty of time to think and plan for another trip. He was truly at peace...

The young man died a few hours later.

Chapter One

A Healthy Skepticism

During ten years of sitting with those who are dying, I have attempted to maintain a healthy skepticism as to what is truth and what is illusion. There is one thing, however, of which I am certain: There is "something", maybe another state of consciousness that exists after physical death. Briefly, here are some of the activities I have witnessed that reinforced my belief.

At some point during the final week of the dying process, there is an eye movement that I call "scanning". The eyes turn upward and move from side to side. This may be a purely physical reaction but in the majority of cases and after this scanning process, the person seems to sleep and there appears to be a calmer, more peaceful look to the face.

During this same period, a certain type of "glaze" covers the eyes yet the person appears to be looking into space and actually seeing "something". While sitting with one client, I very quietly asked if he could tell me what he was viewing. With a faint smile on his face, he answered "No" and continued to look into space. This activity is one that has led me to the belief that the individual is "seeing", maybe even mentally conversing with, other realms of consciousness.

While each case is unique in its progress toward the end of life, there are similarities. All go through periods of intense activity, physical and/or mental, followed by sleep or quietness.

Except in two cases, all died peacefully and calmly; most were not in pain. Whether due to medication or the fact that they were no longer responding to pain stimulus is not known.

I was visiting an African-American lady who was in her late 70's. She appeared calm and peaceful and didn't want to talk. However, she did want me to hold her hand as I had done during previous visits. Near the end, she opened her eyes, looked at me and said, "Sonny. Don't ever let them tell you any different. We are all the same on the inside." And with those words, she died. There are many such lessons to be learned from those whose life is ending. Some can be quite humorous; others can be rather nasty—until the final week. There appears to be a psychological and/or spiritual "turn around" during the final week or even the last few days. It's almost as if the “scanning” and “viewing” periods might be some type of “garbage dumping” process.

One of the humorous incidents occurred when I was asked to visit a young man who was dying of AIDS. I was told he was in the last two or three days of life. When I entered his bedroom, I was confronted with a very good-looking young man in his late 20’s, sitting up in bed, who looked perfectly healthy. Another man was standing at the foot of his bed. Without really thinking, I blurted out, “My but you sure look good today.” His response was to look up at me and, in a nice musical voice, he said, “Oooooh, and so do you.” The man standing at the foot of the bed said, “Well, I see he’s not ready to go yet.” However, within two days this healthy looking young man had deteriorated to “skin and bone” and died peacefully with no more sounds from his lips.

There are a number of sounds made that are, again, unique to each individual passing. They range from talking or not talking to wheezing and the “rattle”. These sounds can be frightening to those around the dying person, but in most cases, they are simply the muscles and nerves responding to a buildup of fluids in the system.

I have visited most clients through a hospice organization. Hospices provide palliative care including as much love and warmth as possible.

Therefore, what I have witnessed may not necessarily be the same as someone who dies in an accident or alone and without medication and other types of care. I wonder if they have that same brief period to look out into what we might interpret as the "void", but what they know as some state of consciousness.

I cannot be more specific as to why I believe as I do but, to my understanding, there are other realms of consciousness that we enter just before and after death.

Matter is spirit in its densest form and
spirit is matter in its highest form.
H. P. Blavatsky
in *The Secret Doctrine*

Chapter Two

Connectedness

He remembered that day, walking away from the doctor's office. He felt as if he was off center, out of balance and out of control of his life. His emotions stung every cell of his being and his mind was spinning with self-destructive and incomplete thoughts. He felt polluted in every part of his being and thought nothing or no one could help him. He felt isolated, alone, separated from everything and everyone. A sense of desperation gripped him with the realization that he was HIV positive.

Now, he was dragging through each day, hoping against hope that something or someone magical would appear to pull him from his state of self-loathing, self-pity and fear. He knew fear was creeping along with him wherever he went. And that's not all. He knew, with certainty, that another crisis was just around the corner waiting to grab him and scream "Gotcha." There was always the sense that another drastic and traumatic incident would finally bring him down. Somehow though the thought, “I can make it just a little while longer. I know I can” would come to his consciousness.

He continued to plod along, feeling dazed and drugged; thinking he was going insane and that his time was almost up. Then a little beam of something—call it light or hope—struck his consciousness and he found himself searching his own mind for solutions. He found hope. HOPE!

How Our Perceptions Empower us.
Or
How Our Perceptions Energize us.

Hope is a type of energy, a pattern in the mind that is activated when you *perceive* a crisis and it is hope that sees you through crises, even when you think there is no hope. Hope pulls you out of that dazed, drugged and polluted sense of being; pollution of body, emotion and mind. Yes, the emotional and mental bodies become polluted just as does the physical body.

Pollution fogs the perceptions. It can be cleared through the use of energies that stem from that vortex of energy called the Higher Self or Soul. The Higher Self, the individual Soul, is part of the larger One Soul; a system within a system. It is energy, in time and space, to be used in crisis resolution so that personal stability can be reestablished.

Why is it that some people continue to plunge through life solving crisis after crisis, apparently stable and with little conflict, and remain happy while you live an unhappy, crisis ridden life? Is it possible that the happy ones have no sense of separation from the Soul, while you have an over developed sense of "me-ness"? "Me-ness" is especially true if you are suffering from an addiction (or two, or three). The book *Alcoholics Anonymous* states, "Selfishness, self-centeredness... is the root of our troubles" (1976, p. 62). To solve a crisis with less conflict, you must learn to move away from self-centeredness, to stand as an observer (Higher Self, the Soul) of your own life and recognize that you have choices. You must understand that you are "driven by a hundred forms of fear, self-delusion, self-seeking, and self-pity" and that your troubles are, in some respects, of your own making *(Ibid.)*.

You may become so stuck in the thinking surrounding your troubles that it becomes necessary to consult professionals to regain your stability. Or, you can use your Soul! Whatever process you use, it helps to remember that interpretations of crises, your perceptions, vary from individual to individual.

You continue to exist because you face and solve crises as a system within larger systems. You encounter crises every day of your life; some small and unimportant, others large and almost incomprehensible. How you encounter and resolves crises depends upon training received from your family, school, friends and other learned influences; your perceptions. It depends also upon the understanding and use of the Higher Self which is, in turn, based upon a concept of spirituality; a belief in something or someone "greater than" that gives you hope of the survival of crises. It is a concept in line with Alice A. Bailey's view of spirituality. She states:

The word "spiritual" relates to attitudes, to relationships, to the moving forward from one level of consciousness to the next. It is related to the power to see a new vision and new and better possibilities. It refers to every effect of the evolutionary process as it drives man forward from one range of sensitivity to another; it relates to expansions of consciousness, to all activity which leads toward some form of further development... Spirituality involves an ever-widening sphere of influence and responsibility (Alice A. Bailey, *The Rays and the Initiations,* p. 364).

The words attitude, relationships and responsibilities provide the key to the resolution of crises and personal stability. What are your perceptions, your attitudes, relationships and responsibilities toward crises, and life in general? Have you learned to escape from the resolution of crises and conflict by using mind-altering chemicals, eating, working, getting lost in TV? What method do you use to face crises and what do you consider a crisis?

What is crisis? The dictionary defines crisis (from the Greek *krisis, krinein)* as separation or sifting. A crisis is a decisive or crucial turning point in a given situation. It can be a time of danger or ease determining whether possible bad or good consequences will follow.

Patterns of thinking, perceptions, attitudes, relationships and responsibilities held in consciousness are the tools with which you solve crises. If these tools are inadequate, you can learn to acquire new ones, and these come about through expansions of consciousness.

You resolve crises through decisive, dynamic and energetic processes that affect a network of systems. Crisis resolution requires a clear mind and emotions, a calm individual system within a larger system, even planetary. The planetary system is a part of the systemic (solar) whole that is a part of a universal (cosmic) whole. The realization that you are a small part in this incomprehensible universe may create a sense of insignificance, fear and hopelessness. However, you contribute to the whole; you are important to the whole. The recognition that your Soul is an available instrument in crisis resolution releases negative emotional states within your individual living systems. This realization helps break down the barriers created by highly emotional reactions and conflicting thought processes; processes that become rituals.

Rituals are processes that, when studied and meditated upon and used, form new frontiers in thinking that lead to expansions of consciousness. These expansions lead you toward new and fulfilling hunting grounds in the realm of crisis resolution. It is not necessary that rituals contain physical movements such as dance or other movement patterns. An act as simple as brushing your teeth every day is a ritual. Simple prayer every day is a ritual. Going to work each day can be interpreted as a ritual. Those unwanted recurring thoughts that plague you are mental rituals. And those recurring emotions that storm your system are emotional rituals.

Six rituals are included in this book. To be truly effective in solving crises and easing the process of dying, a ritual should be learned and **used over a period of years**. However, you can begin now by choosing one ritual to practice each day. More than one ritual should **NOT** be practiced every day since this may create over stimulation of your nervous system. You need calm emotions and a clear mind to perceive possible solutions to crises, not a "bundle of nerves."

Do you perceive crises and emotional/mental change as impassable barriers to life or as crucial and decisive turning points; a door to further opportunity and responsibility? Instead of looking at a crisis as a turning point, it is common to want to separate from it; to run, get away from it as fast as possible. Do you say, "Let someone or something do it for me"; or do you contact your Soul for guidance?

When a solution is not readily available, do you react emotionally; with anger, tears, withdrawal, fear? Do you rely upon clear thinking, sifting through possible choices to make a decision? Do you rely upon your own form of prayer or meditation, your own method of invoking the guidance of spiritual energy, of your Soul?

Whatever method you use to resolve crises, the initial reaction is that of fear, the basic emotion. You face the fear of being without food, clothing, shelter; of being unemployed (or employed); of being loved or not loved and a host of other fears, the most important of which is the fear of dying.

However, before the crisis of death, comes the crisis of birth. Birth (though you do not usually remember it) impacts you dramatically. Then follows a lifetime of facing the crisis of death. The first, birth, separates you from *conscious* unity with your Higher Self and places you in the physical world. The second, death, separates you from the known physical world and places you WHERE? It's that big "where" with which you are confronted, isn't it? There is the fear of the unknown, of where you might be going and what you might become (or not become) after death, if anything or anyone. This is the major crisis of physical life. However, while there may be brief periods of fear, you can resolve the crisis of death, or any other crisis, without long-term fear. Your resolution of crises can be accomplished with acceptance, calmness, peace, even joy.

First, you must release the fear of crisis and change. The release of fear is based on the acceptance of the probability of a positive resolution of each crisis faced. Were it not for crises and change in your life, you would not grow. You can not run from crises or from your thoughts or emotions. The longer you run; the longer you fail to make decisions, rightly or wrongly, the longer you live with stress, conflict and fear.

Second, you must begin to believe something exists that is greater than the physical, emotional and mental systems. Science is accepting more and more, on one level of consciousness or another, the inter-connectedness of all living systems. What is this connectedness? Surely it can't be just the physical connection. What is that "something" that binds all together? Some call it the soul of the individual and of whole. It is not necessary to call it a soul. You can name it a state of being, light, substance or love. You can call it a state, stage or level of consciousness, the Higher Self or the Soul.

If you are inter-connected through something other than the physical apparatus and, if you can accept the fact that life for everyone is a series of transformations and transitions, of crises, then everything and everyone is experiencing similar events at various levels of consciousness. It then becomes a matter of understanding what you were taught and how you can either continue to experience that teaching, if it is positive, or how to change your perceptions if they are negative and fearful.

As an example of crisis resolution, based on experience and training, pause and think of one major crisis you have faced. How did you handle it? What choices surrounded your decision? To what level of consciousness did you turn? You may be in the midst of trying to make an important decision at this very moment. Do you have a personal ritual for resolving crises and calming your mind and emotions? Can you contact your Higher Self, your Soul?

In many instances, you are not taught to solve crises by going within, to your Higher Self, but to deal with them on the level of objectivity; looking to others to solve your problems within the physical, emotional or mental systems. To overcome this problem, you can use a ritual. Rituals are nothing more than a process, used repeatedly, involving the physical, emotional, mental and higher consciousness. Repeated at rhythmic intervals, and when needed, rituals acknowledge and empower you to solve crises and maintain personal stability. Rituals empower the sense of HOPE.

The following ritual illustrates one method of decision making accomplished by contacting your Soul.

Ritual No. 1:

Step 1: Sit comfortably. Close your eyes. Take a deep breath and attempt to feel as relaxed and calm as possible. Imagine somewhere deep within your head that you are making the sound of a humnmmm. This is a place of peace and you feel comfortable and at ease.

Step 2: Imagine a golden balloon (your Soul) above your head. Your Soul is attached to a line of light that is attached to the top of your head. There is a connection between you, the physical being and you, the Soul. Hold that image, visualize it as being your reality and feel comfortable and joyful with the image.

Step 3: Without asking any specific questions, take **one word** as the subject of the crisis with which you are faced. Move it along the line of light up to the Soul. Hold within your Soul the one word theme such as work, career, family, child.

Step 4: Make the following statement, "Let reality govern my every thought, and truth be the master of my life" (Alice A. Bailey, *A Treatise on White Magic*, p. 239).

Step 5: Offer the crisis to your Soul and think, "I reverently demand the presence of guidance through Purpose, Love and Light." Hold that thought for a moment.

Step 6: Visualize information being sent from inside the Soul, slowly moving out of the Soul into the line of light, making its way through the line and into your brain consciousness.

Step 7: Pause for a moment and consider THE PROCESS you experienced.

Summary:

Relax
Sound hummmmm
Visualize golden balloon (your soul)
Connect head to Soul
Choose one word
Send word to Soul
Reality statement
Reverently demand
Hold thought
Visualize information from Soul to brain
Consider the process

You may receive information immediately, or you may not. Be assured though that, at a critical point of decision making, you will somehow know what you must do to solve your particular crisis. Important questions to ask yourself at this point are: Did I experience fear? Did I feel connected with my Higher Self, my Soul? Were there any indications of an active connection? Was there a sense of connection with other Souls or some point of knowingness? If nothing special occurred for you, practice, practice, practice.

Practice builds ritualistic thinking over a period of time (even years or lives) and you cannot expect to reconstruct your personal system of perceptions, your consciousness, by using a new ritual just one time. There are no quick fixes. Through the practice of rituals you make conscious contact with your Soul and conscious contact is the key to crisis resolution and personal stability.

When you perform the foregoing ritual, you are making a conscious contact with energies that are always available to you. These energies transmit information that stem from your inner thought pool of knowledge or you may be drawing upon your Soul, a level of consciousness that is connected to other levels of consciousness or Soul.

The sense of Soul, of intra- and inter-connectedness is acknowledged as a sense of unity, a oneness with The One, whatever your interpretation of The One may be. It is more than just the personality as interpreted by the Western world, a divisive concept. It is more than the "I wants" and "I needs" of everyday life.

A lack of a sense of a Soul, of intra- or inter-connectedness, separatism, is one explanation for what some refer to when using the statement, "I feel as if I have a big hole in me." Separatism occurs when you mentally, emotionally or physically close yourself off from others. When you begin to accept your intra-and inter-connectedness with higher levels of consciousness, you move away from divisive thinking toward a world of unity, the world of Higher Self, Soul, of spirit, of Life. It is within the Soul that you discover you are not alone, that you are ultimately a small system in a vast network of love, light, power, color and sound that permeates the entire cosmos.

Being connected with the network of all Soul assures you that you never really die because the true Soul never dies. It is only the physical shell that returns to the dust of the Earth. It is the true Soul that knows the joy of being part of the ALL, the One Soul. ALL, The One, is another way of indicating a universal living system.

... "points of crisis" are ever succeeded by points of revelation". They might be called "stabilising points of crisis" in which the "occasional becomes the constant and the intended becomes the intentional".

Alice A. Bailey in

Discipleship in the New Age, Vol. II

Chapter Three

The Soul and Crisis

You began physical plane life through the crisis of birth and you discontinue that existence through the process of death. These actions are part of the overall living systems processes. But what of the intervening years?

A review of your life experience will reveal the methods you have used in resolving crises. How did you handle not receiving a special toy you wanted when you were a child? How did you handle your first day at school, your first encounter with a low score on a school test, your first argument with a friend or family member? Were you taught to see the situation as being one involving choices, including the Soul?

You make choices based on physical and emotional desires as well as mental perceptions and intuition of the Soul. Ultimately, whether you accept it or not, the Soul chooses and has the last say in the matter because it has its own plan and purpose. Your Soul institutes the necessary crises in life and moves you forward from one point to another. Also, it is involved in points of crisis in the spiritual realm as well as opportunities for vision, insight and revelation. It is your Soul that provides "the thought of struggle" (Alice A. Bailey, *Discipleship in the New Age, Vol. II,* p. 293).

You focus upon the struggle, forgetting that you can move your attention away from the struggle to the Soul from where you can observe the situation, view alternatives and make decisions. From the level of the Soul, you can become aware of a cleavage or separation between and within your mental and emotional processes; between or within the mental processes and the physical being, or other possible cleavages. These cleavages in consciousness deter you from crisis resolution.

To overcome crises, you follow rules and premises for crisis resolution that often appear contradictory. Some of these rules and premises you can consider and accept "without the aid of a trained psychologist" and train yourself to correct the cleavages. The premises are:

1. We all have psychological difficulties that are universal and not especially unique. The sense of uniqueness brings the tendency to disruptive thinking and loneliness. It makes one part of you too important and this should be counteracted by

seeing your Soul as a whole and integrated system. Uniqueness does not emphasize the Soul but rather the part or parts within the whole.

2. Crisis resolved indicates progress and opportunity, not disaster and failure. You are where you are in life because of crises. In the last analysis, psychological crises are steps that bring the need for effort. Once resolved, there is a sense of gain and of freedom. (Paraphrased from Alice A. Bailey, *Esoteric Psychology, Vol. II,* pp. 427-28).

When you seek someone to help solve a crisis, you are most likely focused on a possible failure. True crisis resolution requires looking at achievements rather than failures, an empowering process.

When opportunity knocks, where are you? Are you wrapped up in emotional reactions to a life bogged down by seeming circumstances, physically tired or ill, or so mentally confused that you can't think straight?

Straight thinking depends upon a clear and uncluttered mind, calm emotions, a relaxed body and conscious contact with your Soul. These requirements are fulfilled by the daily practice of rituals, especially those using the Soul. The following ritual, which involves several states of consciousness, is entitled **Think Blue.**

Ritual No. 2

Explanation: Through experimentation, science has determined that human brain waves function at various cycles per second. The first cycle is the gamma cycle operating from 24 to 48 cycles per second. The color bright red is associated with this cycle and anger, frustration and fighting might be exhibited. The next cycle is from 14 to 24 and is associated with a dull red color. This cycle is recognized as hyperactivity and there may be some anger and loss of objective thinking. At a point approximating 14 cycles per second a situation arises in consciousness that is known as the awareness window. The color green is associated with this window and this is the point at which there is conscious recognition of a crisis situation. From 7 to 14 cycles per second the alpha state of mind is present corresponding to the color blue. This is recognized as calmness, stability and clear thinking. It is the most productive state of mind and is ideal for crisis resolution.

The Process

Step 1: Take several deep breaths, think the number 14 and visualize a dull red color.

Step 2: Count slowly from 14 to 11. As you do so, visualize the color changing slowly from dull red to red-green, then to green.

Step 3: Count slowly from 11 to 7. As you do so, visualize the color green changing slowly to green-blue, then to a peaceful blue.

Step 4: For as long as you can, visualize this peaceful blue color while you maintain the thought of the number seven.

The more you practice this ritual and the sooner you can remember to think the number seven, the sooner the color blue will be associated with that number and you will feel calm physically and emotionally as well as mentally alert.

It is during the alpha state, the blue state, that you can think about and solve your crises. It is while using the alpha state that you can receive information from the Soul about the crisis.

What are these crises? For many people, crises of the personality occur daily, but there are five major crises of the Soul that are important and they take place in the following order:

1. Between the fourth and seventh year, the Soul becomes active through the physical system.

2. During adolescence, the Soul becomes active through the emotional system.

3. Between the twenty-first and twenty-fifth years, the Soul becomes active through the mental system. This is when you begin to respond to the influences of the Soul.

4. Between the thirty-fifth and forty-second years, conscious contact with the Soul can be established if not done so earlier. The personality, as an integrated system, begins to respond to the energies of the Soul.

5. As you mature and expand your consciousness, you can become more aware of the relationship between the Soul and the personality. Finally, around either the fifty-sixth or the sixty-third years, there is a final decision made by the Soul as to whether you continue to grow or decline toward the end of life. The outcome of this crisis determines how you will use your energies and

forces for the remaining years of your life. (Alice A. Bailey, *Esoteric Psychology,* pp. 53-54).

These are the major crises of the Soul, but there are lesser cycles of both the personality and the Soul. Maintaining a higher vision reduces the stress connected with crises.

It is the recognition and acceptance of the interconnectedness of the underlying consciousness that enables you to understand crises, especially the crisis of physical death.

Can you view the dying process as part of the on-going crises of the Soul? When you practice Soul rituals, you are preparing your Soul for the release of the fear surrounding death and the dying process as well as crisis resolution in general. Crisis resolution returns you to a state of stability or near-equilibrium, peace and calmness.

The overcoming of death is not contingent upon the elimination of bodily ills, but upon the establishing of that continuity of consciousness which carries over from the physical plane of life to the inner subjective existence.

Alice A. Bailey in
Externalization of the Hierarchy

Chapter Four

Consciousness

Near-equilibrium relates to consciousness that relates not only to current physical plane existence, but to those states of consciousness known as "life after death", "rebirth" or "reincarnation". The fact of rebirth has been a part of religious and philosophical beliefs for centuries. As late as 553 A.D., the Christian Church practiced this belief. According to M. V. Kamath, in *The Philosophy of Death and Dying,* at the Second Council of Constantinople one-third of the bishops voted for the doctrine of reincarnation and two-thirds voted against it. He indicates that the doctrine probably conflicted with assumed priestly powers to remit sins (1978, p. 60).

What actually occurred to change the minds of two-thirds of the voters may never be known, but you can bet your sweet bippy that it probably had to do with money and power. [Wups! A personal cleavage found its way into my consciousness]. Whether it was money, power or some other reason, no doubt the decision had to do with polluted consciousness.

How do you experience states of consciousness? Do you find yourself daydreaming? Are there times when you find you have been spaced out? When you are highly emotional, are you aware of your mental activity or the activity of the Soul?

What is your mind and the Soul doing at the times of emotional upheavals? Are you conscious of your mental activity? A basic fact from the Ageless Wisdom is energy follows and conforms to thought.

Where are your thoughts sending their energy? When you speak to someone are you not directing mental, emotional (even physical) energy toward the other person? Doesn't a minister or priest direct spiritual energy through the mind and voice to the congregation?

Energy direction is implied by the ancient Delphic injunction "Know thyself." Are you using your energies for crisis resolution and better relationships or for strictly selfish purposes? If you are using them for the latter, then you are experiencing a lack of conscious contact with the Soul that may be due to physical, emotional or mental pollution. This leads to chaos and crises.

Is your life chaotic and crisis ridden without any understanding of what is occurring or any hope of resolution? If your physical, emotional and mental life are constantly polluted, the use of rituals can help you achieve clarity. However, remember that rituals can create crises because you are bringing unconscious patterns and perceptions into your consciousness. If your physical, emotional and mental systems are maintained in a clear state of consciousness, your crises will be solved with little or no stress and confusion.

To help maintain stability and clarity, use the following ritual that can be completed in about 30 seconds.

Ritual No. 3

Step 1: Take a deep breath. As you exhale, make a humming sound (can be done soundlessly if necessary) and feel your physical body relax.

Step 2: Visualize yourself standing in a clear, crystal globe which extends to about elbow length, as if your arms are stretched out (this is the emotional system). Inhale deeply, breath out with a hum and maintain the crystal clear visualization.

You can take this ritual a step further for mental clarity.

Step 3: Visualize a space above your head as being crystal clear and completely calm. Again use the breathing and humming process.

If you perform this ritual with regularity, in full consciousness of what you are doing, you are beginning to establish conscious contact with the Soul. You are learning how to use the energies of your Soul.

Know thou... that there never was a time
when I, nor thou,... was
not; nor shall there ever come a time
...when any of us shall cease to be.
Bhagavad Gita,
The Song of God

Chapter Five

Death

The practice of attempting to maintain near-equilibrium and attain conscious soul contact throughout physical life was confirmed by Plato. According to Edward F. Edinger in *Anatomy of the Psyche,* Plato believed we can train ourselves to be conscious of a state similar to death. Then, when death does come, it will not present a problem (1985, p. 170).

This does not imply that you must become morbid in thinking about death or that you should dwell on the probability. Rituals, in conjunction with daily meditation, will help establish a pattern of thought that will allow you to see death as a transition, a physical plane crisis maybe but a transition, a continuation of consciousness into the realm of Soul.

To simulate this transition, use the following ritual. **It is important to understand that this ritual will not end your physical life and this fact cannot be stressed too much; it is a ritual simulating a state of consciousness.**

Ritual No. 4

Step 1: Close your eyes, take a deep breath and attempt to feel as relaxed and calm as possible. Imagine somewhere deep within your head that you are making the sound of a hummmm. This is a place of peace and you feel comfortable and at ease.

Step 2: Imagine a golden balloon (the Soul) just above your head. Your Soul is attached to a line of light that is attached to the top of your head. There is a connection between you, the physical being and you, the spiritual being. Hold that image, visualize it as being your reality and feel comfortable and joyful with the image.

Step 3: Lift your consciousness upward confirming that your being is in the center of the golden balloon.

Step 4: Visualize a tiny pin hole in the top of balloon where the light is slowly, peacefully and joyfully escaping through it. See the escaping light as all the excess you have carried with you throughout life whatever you view as excess.

Step 5: As the light escapes, visualize your individual Soul becoming aware of other realms of consciousness and feel a sense of extreme clarity, of connectedness because all the excess garbage you have carried is being slowly transformed into spiritual energy.

Step 6: Visualize the line of light extending from the top of the balloon to infinity and know that infinity as your spiritual home and that someone is waiting for you.

Step 7: Feel joyous anticipation and expectation as you visualize the light dissolving into a realm of rainbow colors, peace, unity and joy.

When using the above ritual, as well as any other ritual, practicality and simplicity should be considered along with motive or purpose. Rituals do not have to be fanciful, though some people may need fancy ceremonies to gain a fuller understanding of other states of consciousness.

The simpler the ritual, the easier it is for the mind to interpret new ideas coming from the Soul. And the Soul knows. It knows its time and its rhythm. The Soul has its own plan, its time of entering and its time of departure from the three dimensional plane of consciousness. This plane includes two aspects established at the time of birth. The Soul, or consciousness aspect, enables you to be a rational, thinking person. The other aspect, the life aspect, is that which holds all your parts together and, like an electrical current, keeps you alive and active.

You become aware of these aspects through meditation, study and service. Meditation, a type of ritual, is the most effective means by which you can discover these aspects. They are interwoven with the one great aspect of the planet, even the solar system.

Therefore, constant effort at conscious contact with the Soul, with the One Life, continued over time, prepares you for eventual physical departure. This may be more of an undefined sensing rather than a concrete thought. If your Soul knows its own time and if you have the means, the mind, to sense this, you can bring the two together to be fully prepared for your own time of departure from the physical plane.

It is the physical plane, is it not, with which you are concerned; the physical body? However, the physical body is transitory and impermanent; it is not the same from one moment to the next (Kamath, *The Philosophy of Death and Dying,* 1978, p. 58).

From one moment to the next, as your physical body ages, it is in the process of deterioration, preparing for the final crisis. It is the physical body upon which focus and importance is placed, but if you can learn to relinquish the physical body, in consciousness, to your Soul, then peace is gained. The physical form will stay together as long as your dynamic thought power holds it together (Alice A. Bailey, *A Treatise on White Magic,* p. 554).

Are you, at this point of reading, becoming depressed at the possible loss of your physical body; or, are you beginning to grasp that there is something greater—the larger, all-encompassing Soul? You are part of the larger Soul and you are connected with all that exists and that includes your fellow human beings.

If you are connected with all that is, the One Soul, is it not possible to understand that you, the essential you, the individual Soul never dies? Plato believed in the fact of the soul (the Self) and its long journey through eternity. He believed that there are three parts to the soul. One part is immortal or rational and comes from God. A second part is mortal or animal and is sensitive because it is the seat of the appetites and the sensations. A third part is between the other two and makes interaction possible. He called this middle part will or spirit that is used to overcome desire.

While there are those who believe in the fact of the Soul and its functions, there are many who, unlike Plato, are skeptical of the idea. Science approves and disapproves. With all the scientific and spiritual knowledge available, there must be a better method of preparing for death. Hospice programs are available to help in the final months of the dying process.

Elisabeth Kűbler-Ross devotes her book, *On Death and Dying,* to the fear and denial surrounding death. The major fear is that of taking into the after-life accumulated resentments, hatreds and angers—of "going to hell".

Do you want to die with resentments, hatred, anger, fear; or, with a loving and forgiving heart? Can you forgive yourself and others? At this point in human evolution it is probably impossible for the average person to be completely free of such emotions and thoughts. However, you can begin now to prepare for death.

You can begin the process by accepting that you are an integral part of the One Life and by learning about forgiveness of your fellow human being. *A Course in Miracles* puts it this way:

"If your brothers are part of you, will you accept them? Only they can teach you what you are, for your learning is the result of what you

taught them. What you call upon in them you call upon in yourself. And as you call upon it in them it becomes real to you... If what you do to my brother you do to me, and if you do everything for yourself because we are part of you, everything we do belongs to you as well. Everyone God created is part of you and shares His glory with you. His Glory belongs to Him, but it is equally yours. You cannot, then, be less glorious than He is." (1975/1985, T. 174).

The idea that you are your brother's keeper has been around for centuries, but it is still a difficult concept for many to accept.

The following ritual is provided as a possible process to find your Soul, a point of spiritual power; to recognize your Soul as part of other Souls and to help you find your center in the midst of the One Life. Whatever you visualize or imagine during this process is yours. There is no right or wrong. What's yours, is yours!

Ritual No. 5

You are standing in the middle of a room, facing a doorway. The door opens and you walk through it onto a porch. In front of you are three steps and you step down them into a gravel path. As you move along the gravel path, you can feel the gravel under your feet and hear the crunching sound.

At the end of the path is a field of grass and flowers. As you move through the field, you are aware of the many different colors and scents of the flowers and you feel them lightly brush against your legs. At the edge of the field you see three large trees. These trees are your own personal trees, whatever type you wish them to be. You walk to the trees and feel their bark.

You sense their strength and hear the rustle of their leaves blowing gently in the wind. You move between the trees and walk to a small brook.

Standing at the edge, you look down into the clear, sparkling water. You can see the rocks at the bottom as the water ripples gently over them. You might even bend down and put your fingers in the water. Is it cool, warm, cold?

As you stand upright you are aware of two paths, one to the left and one to the right. You decide to take the right hand path and find yourself moving up a slight hill. As you move upward, you feel a sense of lightness and you are breathing comfortably and evenly.

When you reach the top of the hill, you see the entrance to a cave before you. In its dimness you are aware of a small light somewhere within and you decide to investigate.

As you walk through the cave, you feel safe and secure. You feel a gentle breeze moving over your body.

You arrive at the light and discover it to be a candle placed on a stone shelf. In front of the shelf is a stone seat and you decide to sit on it. It feels comfortable and as you settle onto it, you are aware that the candle is level with your eyes. You are experiencing the light in the cave of your heart. You feel at peace and calm. As you look at the candle, a pure white light grows from it and gradually surrounds you. You feel this light as calming, peaceful; something safe and secure. You are aware that this pure white light is the light of spiritual love and it moves around and through you, filling you with a peace and comfort you may never have felt before. As you sit calmly in this pure white light, you realize it is your inner spirit, your contact with whatever you see as your personal God. You know that here you can ask any question, and with faith, receive your answer.

For a brief period, about one minute, as you feel the pure white light of love around and within you, ponder on the question you would like answered.

You are aware now that the light has grown smaller and returned to the candle on the shelf. Feeling at peace and serene, and very rested, you arise and move out of the cave. You move back down the hill and, as you do, you can see the brook, the trees, the field of flowers and your own particular room in the distance.

You pass the brook, hearing its gurgling sound much clearer, almost musical. You pass beneath your trees, feeling their strength surge through you, and you move into the field. As you walk through it, you can see the colors more vividly, smell their scents more strongly.

You are on the gravel path and can feel the gravel under your feet, hear the crunching sound much clearer than before.

You walk up the steps, across the porch, open the door and enter the room, turning once again to face the door. You feel complete, whole, serene, joyous and a part of the total cosmos. You know that anytime you need an answer from your own center, you can come to this inner place and find it. You know that you can also find that inner sense of togetherness, of wholeness, within the pure white light.

FOOTNOTE: A highly recommended book is *Unconditional Love and Forgiveness* by Edith C. Stauffer, Ph.D., available from Triangle Publishers and distributed by Psychosynthesis International, P. O. Box 926, Diamond Springs, CA 95619.

I am going to close my terrestrial eyes but my spiritual eyes will remain open, wider than ever.

Victor Hugo in

A Philosophy of Death and Dying

Chapter Six

It's the Law

Resolving crises involves the use energies. The qualities or energies of the human system, as part of larger systems, are governed by planetary, solar and universal laws. The major law that applies to our planet and humanity states that all disease is the result of inhibited life of the Soul. Disease is a crisis of either short or long duration and, esoterically, disease is seen as the product of and results from three influences:

1. Your past (as you sew, so shall you reap)

2. That which you have inherited; and,

2. The result of the activities of natural forms

(Alice A. Bailey, *Esoteric Healing,* p. 544).

Disease, as a distorted reflection of divine possibilities both physical and psychological, stems from the beautiful and the true. These possibilities are energy because all is energy stemming from the Life of the One Soul. The conflict of energies with forces produces disease. Right interaction of energies and forces allows for the energies of the Soul to be active within, through and around your body. This produces good health and right activity.

Good health depends upon the unimpeded flow of energy and its related action to corresponding glands within your physical body. When the relationship between energies and glands is interrupted, disease results. If not corrected, disease eventually results in death.

The crises of disease and death result from the will of the Soul and the "magnetic power of the planetary life." Will can withdraw the life essence, bringing about the process of death. The atomic structure of the planetary life may reabsorb all within its sphere (Alice A. Bailey, *Esoteric Healing,* pp. 534-35).

Absorption (death) and birth are cyclic and continue until "perfection calls imperfection to the surface." At points along the great cyclic chain, your Soul tells the form that it has completed its purpose for the current cycle. The mind becomes aware of this process and the form responds dropping away. The Soul is free *(Ibid).*

The preceding comments provide clues to the cause of crisis, disease and death. Medical and holistic practices attempt to conquer disease and rituals abound to honor death. What of the actual dying process itself? Can there be a ritual for dying? A technique? Eastern psychology indicates there was (and is) a technique for dying but it has been lost in the West (Alice A. Bailey, A *Treatise on White Magic,* p. 302). Additionally, there is information covering "a newer and more scientific method of handling the process of dying" (Ibid., p. 499). The hints, clues and information presented here should be implemented along with sound modern medical science. When pain has subsided (and there does come that point) and the body is weakened, you should be permitted, "even if apparently unconscious", to prepare for the great transition termed death *(Ibid.,* pp. 502-07).

Can you imagine a time when instead of tears and fear and the refusal of the inevitable, the dying person and his family and friends would agree on a time for death to occur. Nothing but happiness would then characterize the dying process (Alice A. Bailey, *A Treatise on White Magic,* pp. 499-500).

The East has established certain rituals to help prepare for the process of death. There are four basic rules for the transition and while they may appear simplistic, they are effective.

First, through the daily practice of visualization and meditation, you can learn the process of keeping focused in the head center. This increases your capacity to "live increasingly as the king seated on the throne between the eyebrows." You can use this process in everyday affairs.

Second, learn to help others from the energy of the heart. By so doing, you learn to transcend emotionalism and to recognize that you are actually helping a unit within a system, the larger group. When serving with the group in mind, you must determine if your motive is directed from your soul or if it is from selfish ambition and a desire to stand out.

Third, when falling asleep, you can practice withdrawing your consciousness into the head center. This allows you to move your consciousness to the dream state. Until this withdrawing process is learned, you simply drift off to sleep.

Fourth, keep a diary of all phenomena connected with both the daily practice of withdrawing and meditation. Daily meditation is the key to learning conscious control of your energies and forces related to the process of dying; or, any other crisis (Alice A. Bailey, *A Treatise on White Magic,* pp. 502-07).

As to the actual dying process, there should be silence in the room of the individual making the transition. When silence is observed "the departing soul can hold possession of its instrument with clarity until the last minute and can make due preparation." This is because the dying person may "appear" to be unconscious but is, in reality, conscious *(Ibid.).*

When more is learned about death in connection with color, a ceremony will be held and orange lights will be placed in the death room. This is done when no recovery is possible and "aids the focusing in the head." In addition to color, and when sound is better understood, music and mantric phrases will be used *(Ibid.).* Other suggestions include placing the dying person's head symbolically toward the East, the feet and hands crossed, and sandalwood incense burned.

These rules and processes will be part of the Science of Death "only when the fact of the soul is recognized and its relation to the body has been scientifically demonstrated" (Alice A. Bailey, *A Treatise on White Magic,* pp. 502-07). The Ageless Wisdom encourages us to "push the study of death and its technique as far as possible and to carry forward... investigation of this matter" *(Ibid.)*.

Rituals, similar but different, have been presented. They function as dynamic and effective processes for crisis resolution. Practicing these rituals can empower you to take control of your life, to move outward, upward or inward, thus becoming the Observer or Soul of your own life processes.

You can learn to make conscious contact with your Soul and live a life of relative peace and joy. Joy can be experienced, even during the transition of death, because completing a purpose is always joyful. Death is the completion of purpose.

You and your loved ones may experience a sense of loss during crises and/or the death process. However, if you accept the underlying interaction of consciousness as an on-going, never-ending process, you are more empowered to find solutions to life's crises and experience the joy of your soul.

In conclusion, only one thing more can be added to the information presented in this book - the final ritual which is a modification of **Ritual No. 4.**

Ritual No. 6

Step 1: Close your eyes, take a deep breath and attempt to feel as relaxed and calm as possible. Imagine somewhere deep within your head that you are making the sound of a hummmmm. This is a place of peace for you and you feel comfortable and at ease.

Step 2: Imagine a golden balloon (your Soul) just above your head. Your Soul is attached to a line of light that is attached to the top of your head. There is a connection between you, the physical being and you, the spiritual being. Hold that image, visualize it as being your reality and feel comfortable and joyful with the image.

Step 3: Lift your consciousness upward confirming that your being is in the center of the soul.

Step 4: Visualize a point of white light about three inches in front of and between the eyes.

Step 5: Visualize a point of blue light about three inches from the back between the shoulder blades.

Step 6: Visualize the white light moving from between the eyes to the center of the soul.

Step 7: Visualize the blue light moving from between the shoulder blades to the center of the soul.

Step 8: Visualize a tiny pin hole in the top of your Soul through which the light is slowly, peacefully and joyfully escaping. See the escaping light as if it contains all the excess you have carried with you throughout life, whatever you view as excess.

Step 9: As the light escapes, visualize your Soul beginning to dissolve slowly and feel a sense of extreme clarity, of connectedness.

Step 10: Visualize the line of light extending from the top of your soul to infinity and know infinity as your spiritual home and that someone is waiting for you.

Step 11: Feel joyous anticipation and expectation as you visualize the line of light slowly dissolving into a realm of rainbow colors, peace, unity and joy. Someone takes your hand and

Welcome Home!

References

Bailey, Alice A. (1934/1951). *A Treatise on White Magic,* New York: Lucis Publishing Company. (1955).

Discipleship in the New Age, Vol. II. (1953). New York: Lucis Publishing Company.

Esoteric Healing. (1942/1970). New York: Lucis Publishing Company.

Esoteric Psychology, Vol. II. (1960). New York: Lucis Publishing Company.

The Rays and the Initiations. (1930/1965). New York: Lucis Publishing Company.

The Soul and Its Mechanism. (1930). New York: Lucis Publishing Company.

Edinger, E. F. (1985). *Anatomy of the Psyche.* LaSalle, IL: Open Court.

Kamath, M. V. (1978). *The Philosophy of Death and Dying,* Honesdale, PA: Himalayan International Institute of Yoga Science and Philosophy

Kűbler-Ross, E. (1969). *On Death and Dying,* New York: MacMillan Publishing. (1975/1985).

A Course in Miracles, Foundation for Inner Peace, P. O. Box 1104, Glen Ellen, CA 95442. (1976).

Alcoholics Anonymous, 3rd Edition, A. A. World Services, Inc., 475 Riverside Drive, New York, NY 10115

Notes

Notes

Notes

Notes

Notes

Notes

Notes

Notes

About the Author

Ford Boyer, co-author of *Listening to the Soul,* earned a Certification in Addiction Studies, a BA in Liberal Arts and an MA in Interdisciplinary Consciousness Studies from John F. Kennedy University. He earned also a Doctor of Divinity degree from the American Bible Institute, a diploma in Metaphysical Theology from Holy Well Bible College and is an ordained minister. He has studied Eastern philosophies for over 30 years and synthesizes East and West thinking in his efforts to establish right human relations. Being semi-retired, Ford edits, writes for, and publishes *Starfire*, a bi-monthly esoteric psychology/philosophy newsletter with an international distribution. He currently resides with his wife in the San Francisco Bay Area. His web site address is:

http://starserve.home.attbi.com.

www.ingramcontent.com/pod-product-compliance
Ingram Content Group UK Ltd.
Pitfield, Milton Keynes, MK11 3LW, UK
UKHW041821200726
13854UKWH00001BA/258

9 780759 654877